LAUGHTER IS THE BEST MEDICINE
So if you meet somebody with broken ribs, make sure to tickle them.
© Jim Benton

WHEN LIFE GIVES YOU LEMONS...
use them to squirt lemon juice into the eyes of your enemies.
© Jim Benton

ANYBODY WHO SAYS YOU ONLY HAVE YOURSELF TO BLAME...
is just not very good at blaming other people.
© Jim Benton

NEVER BE ASHAMED OF YOUR MOOD SWINGS.
I mean, who doesn't love swings?
© Jim Benton

THE VOICES IN YOUR HEAD ARE NOT REAL.
But they still have some really great ideas.
© Jim Benton

EXERCISE HARD. EAT RIGHT.
Die anyway.
© Jim Benton

What?
IF YOU CAN'T SAY SOMETHING NICE,
don't say anything at all... unless it's about somebody who can't hear you.
© Jim Benton

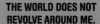
THE WORLD DOES NOT REVOLVE AROUND ME.
It's the whole stupid universe that revolves around me.
© Jim Benton

LEARN THE DIFFERENCE BETWEEN RIGHT AND WRONG.
You'll probably choose wrong, but you should at least know which is which.
© Jim Benton

© Jim Benton

WE MUST NEVER, EVER BE MEAN TO STUPID PEOPLE.
If we are, they might go away. Then who will we laugh at?

ME
THERE'S NO "I" IN TEAM.
But there's a "me."
© Jim Benton

THE BEST THINGS IN LIFE ARE FREE.
Or at least they're on sale.
© Jim Benton

LIKE FATHER, LIKE SON.
How sad is that for Mom?

© Jim Benton

DON'T COUNT YOUR CHICKENS BEFORE THEY'RE HATCHED.
But you can count your eggs.

© Jim Benton

© Jim Benton
LOVE MAKES THE WORLD GO 'ROUND.
But I'm pretty sure money has something to do with it, too.

THE BEST THINGS IN LIFE ARE FREE.
Or at least they're on sale.

© Jim Benton

THE PEN IS MIGHTIER THAN THE SWORD.
If we are talking about, like, a two-inch-long sword.

© Jim Benton

DON'T JUDGE A BOOK BY ITS COVER.
Judge it by how many pictures it has in it.

© Jim Benton

CURIOSITY KILLED THE CAT.
I think we gave that rottweiler a bad attitude by naming him Curiosity.

© Jim Benton

BETTER LATE THAN NEV
I'll finish that tomorrow.

© Jim Benton

THOSE WHO LIVE IN GLASS HOUSES SHOULDN'T THROW STONES.
And they shouldn't walk around in their underwear either.

© Jim Benton

YOU CAN'T HAVE YOUR CAKE AND EAT IT TOO.
But you CAN have your cake and eat someone else's cake too. And that's kind of better, anyway.

© Jim Benton

TWO WRONGS DON'T MAKE A RIGHT.
It takes more like five or six wrongs.

© Jim Benton

YOU CAN HELP ANYONE TURN THAT FROWN UPSIDE DOWN!
Just pull off their head and flip it over.

© Jim Benton

it's happy bunny™

Life. Get One.

NO ACTUAL BUNNIES WERE PHYSICALLY HARMED OR
EMOTIONALLY DAMAGED IN THE MAKING OF THIS BOOK
(THOUGH ONE CHICKEN DID SUSTAIN MINOR INJURIES).

ANY WISDOM ONE GETS FROM A BUNNY IS PROBABLY
NOT THAT HOT. FOR YOUR OWN SAFETY, PLEASE DO
NOT TAKE THE ADVICE OF BUNNIES.

it's happy bunny™

Life. Get One.

And other words of wisdom and junk
that will make you wise or something.

By Jim Benton

SCHOLASTIC INC.

New York   Toronto   London   Auckland   Sydney
Mexico City   New Delhi   Hong Kong   Buenos Aires

For Cindy Levitt and Karen Kiefaber, who did their share to help It's Happy Bunny get a life, and as always, for Griffin, Summer, and Mary K.

ISBN-13: 978-0-545-00827-3
ISBN-10: 0-545-00827-1

12 11 10 9 8 7 6 5 4 3 2 1   8 9 10 11 12 13/0

This edition first printing, April 2008

So, you want to get wise,
do you?

Well, you could read Confucius or Socrates. You could study Solomon or Plato. But only one form of wisdom really and truly has a lot of pictures of bunnies. . . .

Chapter 1
Ancient Bunny Wisdom

The world
does not revolve
around me.

It's the whole
stupid universe
that revolves
around me.

There's no "I" in team.

But there's a "me."

Love makes the
world go 'round.

But I'm pretty sure money has something to do with it, too.

Work hard and the world is your oyster.
Yup, you get a big, snotty oyster-scented world.

You can help anyone turn a
frown upside down!

Just pull off their head
and flip it over.

Do unto others as you would have them do unto you.

Unless, of course, they did unto you first, and now you have to totally open a can of "unto" on them.

Laughter is the best medicine.

So if you meet somebody with broken ribs, make sure to tickle them.

We must never, ever be mean
to stupid people.

If we are, they might go away.
Then who will we laugh at?

Learn the difference
between right and wrong.

You'll probably choose wrong,
but you should at least know
which is which.

When life gives you lemons . . .

. . . use them to squirt lemon
juice into the eyes of
your enemies.

I was sad because I had no shoes, until I met a man who had no feet.

And I said, "Hey, Footless
Dude, guess you won't mind
if I take your shoes."

. . . for example, the most
horrible farts can be
used to inflate the most
beautiful balloons.

Anybody who says you only
have yourself to blame . . .

. . . is just not very good at
blaming other people.

Quiz Time!

Okay, you've been on the path to Enlightenment now for 27 pages. Let's see if you're any closer.

Is the glass half empty or half full?

A) Half empty.

B) Half full.

C) I like pancakes and ducks.

Answer: The correct answer is C. Sometimes the key to wisdom is not to answer every stupid question that somebody asks you.

Fables teach valuable lessons, like *let Grandma get her own basket of goodies*. Read this one, and see how much smarter it makes you.

Chapter 2

The Fable of the Excellent Bunny

Once there was this excellently perfect bunny (like you).

The bunny always did perfectly excellent things.

One day the bunny
met this chicken
who was a huge jerk.

And this chicken always did mean horrible things.

The excellent bunny
wanted to make friends
with the jerk chicken.

punt

But as you know, there's no
talking to jerks like that.

So the bunny let his friend,
Mr. Bear, eat the chicken.

And then everything was great!

Moral

All problems
can be solved
by letting a bear
eat them.

Quiz Time!

Let's see if you
truly understand
the moral of
the story.

After I read "The Fable of
the Excellent Bunny"
I felt:

A) The need to acquire a bear.

B) Alarm over the number of people
   I know who have recently acquired
   their own bears.

C) Swindled out of the cost of this book.

Answer: The incorrect answer is C.

Wow. Enlightenment
sure is *heavy*. Let's take
some time out for
Fun & Games.

Chapter 3
Fun & Games

The path to Enlightenment
is tricky. Can you find
your way?

France

Dorktucky

Idiotapolis

BONEHEADVILLE

Stupidness

Moronto

Enlightenment

Spazistan

Never judge people.
Until you know how.

	Totally Great Looking	Good Looking	Okay Looking
Total Genius	Let's be serious. Except for you and me, there is no such person as this.	You will have one teacher like this and wonder why they don't have a better job.	Could be a scientist. Could be a turnip farmer. Could **not** be a pro athlete.
Smart	This is the person you want to date.	These people run the world, so just watch it.	Most doctors seem to come in about here.
Bright	This person would make a great movie star.	This is the person you should date.	This person almost always thinks that they are one level better than this.
Normal	This person would make a great recording star.	A good car salesperson.	This is what your friends will think of the person you date.
Kind of Stupid	This person would make a great TV weather forecaster.	You will date this person and wonder every day why you do.	This is most of your neighbors.
Total Idiot	This person would be a great model, and you can pay them in coloring books instead of cash.	Will probably star in a commercial for disposable razors.	Sooner or later, you will have this person for a boss.

Just pick someone you know. Then figure out how ugly they are across the top, and how stupid they are down the side.

Plain	Kind of Ugly	Totally Ugly	
So smart that they may actually be ugly, but being this smart makes them seem better looking.	Will invent half of the things in your house.	Will wind up as one of the best people that ever lived.	**Total Genius**
This person would be a great friend. Too bad you'll never notice them.	Good person to call with your computer questions.	Good person to have water your plants while you're away. (NOT feed the cat, which they might scare.)	**Smart**
Everybody has a best friend **exactly** like this.	Sooner or later, you will probably have a crush you can't explain on this person.	This person could be a huge movie star playing the bad guy.	**Bright**
This is most of the people and yogurt in the world, and all things considered, about all you can hope for.	This person spends a lot of time trying to get up to "plain."	This person is just happy they're not as stupid as they could be.	**Normal**
This is what your brother will think of the person you date.	This is probably how you see most of your family. But don't feel guilty. It's how they see you, too.	A perfect friend! They think you're gorgeous and are totally impressed when you just tie your shoes.	**Kind of Stupid**
This is the person your best friend will date.	This is what your sister will think of the person you date.	Don't be too hard on this person. One horse kick to the face and this is you.	**Total Idiot**

Now that you've judged others,
wouldn't it be fun to judge yourself?

Are You Good or Evil?

Maybe you're a blessing. Maybe you're a curse.
Take this quick personality quiz and find out.

1. It's Grandpa's birthday. What would you like to get him?

   a. I'd like to get him a car.

   b. I'd like to get him some medicine. He seems to like that.

   c. I'd like to get him locked up.

2. You find a purse full of money. What would you do?

   a. I'd organize a huge search to find the rightful owner.

   b. I'd take it to the police and let them handle it.

   c. Purse? What purse? I never saw any purse.

3. Your little brother wants some of your candy bar.
   What would you do?

   a. I'd give him the candy and trust him to split it and give me half.

   b. I'd split it and give him half.

   c. I'd split it so he thought he was getting some, and then I'd eat both halves as his howls of jealous rage enhanced the delicious sweetness of the moment.

4. Your aunt, who is, like, 100 years old, asks you if you think a face-lift would help her appearance. What would you say?

   a. "Don't be silly. You're absolutely gorgeous."

   b. "That's really up to you, Auntie, but I think you look fine."

   c. "Would a face-lift help? I don't think a forklift would help."

5. There's a baby bird sitting in the path of an oncoming bus. What would you do?

   a. Risk my life by diving to save the baby bird.

   b. Stay on the sidewalk and yell to the bus driver, "Stop! Stop!"

   c. Check and see if I have any maple syrup in my backpack for the baby bird pancake I'm about to enjoy.

Scoring your answers:

IF YOU ANSWERED MOSTLY C, start growing out your bangs now. You'll want them to conceal the horns that will be sprouting soon.

IF YOU ANSWERED MOSTLY B, you're a normal, average person. But in spite of that, you're good.

IF YOU ANSWERED MOSTLY A, you're so good that you're practically an angel. Either that or you're a big phony and a huge liar, and that makes you the most evil of all.

Bonus Fun!

Write a letter of apology to yourself.

Before your journey can truly be complete,
you have to forgive yourself for errors
you've made along the way.

But let's not take all day or anything.

Use this letter as a simple guide.
Figure out what you want to say to yourself,
circle the red words that are appropriate,
and you'll be on your way.

Dear Self,

Sorry I made those bad **decisions** **choices** **counterfeits**. I know now that even though I was always sure I had good **intentions** **motives** **accomplices**, I needed to spend some more time thinking about how my actions would appear **to family** **to friends** **on the security camera**.

Some might find this hard to believe, but you know all I ever really wanted was to be **loved** **rich** **acquitted**. I guess I just keep hoping that one day the entire world will understand **me** **English**.

I promise that from now on, I won't worry all the time about losing **weight** **friends** **the police** and I'll try to be the best person I can be, although I can't promise that I won't make an occasional **mistake** **enemy** **prison break**.

I'm also going to go easier on the people around me, because I understand now that deep down they really and truly **love me** **care about me** **will file charges**.

I know that you forgive me.

_____

(Sign your name)

Quiz Time!

Look carefully
and see if you can
tell which two are
exactly alike.

Congratulations!

You are now officially ready
to Have a Life!

Take good care of it, and
don't tell the idiots you
have one or they'll want
to get their grimy
paws all over it.

Here are a few nuggets
of wisdom to take with
you as you go.

Chapter 4

One order of nuggets to go.

You can't have your
cake and eat it too.

But you *can* have your
cake and eat someone else's
cake too, and that's kind of
better, anyway.

Exercise hard. Eat right.
Die anyway.

If you can't say something nice, don't say anything at all.

Unless it's about somebody who can't hear you.

Never be ashamed of
your mood swings.

I mean, who doesn't
love swings?

the voices in
your head
are not real.

but they still
have some
really great
ideas.

And finally, always remember:
You can choose your friends, but
you can't choose your family.

But you *can* choose the insane asylum where you have them all put away.

TWO WRONGS DON'T MAKE A RIGHT.

It takes more like
five or six wrongs.

THE PEN IS MIGHTIER
THAN THE SWORD.

If we are talking about, like,
a two-inch-long sword.

DON'T JUDGE A BOOK BY ITS COVER.

Judge it by how many pictures it has in it.

THE BEST THINGS IN LIFE
ARE FREE.

Or at least they're on sale.

BETTER LATE THAN NEV

I'll finish that tomorrow.

ALL GOOD THINGS MUST
COME TO AN END.

But school does, too.

THOSE WHO LIVE
IN GLASS HOUSES
SHOULDN'T
THROW STONES.

And they shouldn't walk around
in their underwear either.

Collect signatures from
your friends, so when
you forget them later . . .
you can remember who
to make fun of.